Published in 2020 by Connor Court Publishing Pty Ltd

Copyright © Cath La Rosa (text), Victoria Carlsund (illustrations) Australia 2020

All rights reserved. No part of this book may be reproduced or transmitted in any form or by any means, electronic or mechanical, including photocopying, recording or by any information storage and retrieval system, without prior permission in writing from the publisher.

Connor Court Publishing Pty Ltd
PO Box 7257
Redland Bay QLD 4165

sales@connorcourt.com
www.connorcourtpublishing.com.au
Phone 0497 900 685

ISBN: 9781922449245

Scripture: New International Readers version – Kidz Bibles – Zonderkidz

Front Cover Design: Maria Giordano

Printed in Australia

"God's gifts of grace come in many forms. Each of you has received a gift in order to serve others. You should use it faithfully."
(1 Peter 4:10)

Gifts

Written by Cath La Rosa
Illustrated by Victoria Carlsund

Connor Court Publishing

Billy Bilby was so excited. His school was going to be having a visit with some people that live in aged care.

They were people just like his Grandma and Grandpa. Billy loved to spend time with people. He loved to talk with them and hear stories about their lives.

Billy's teacher said that they were going to be giving gifts to the older people. Billy thought about this long and hard. What gifts could he buy for these special people? How do you even buy a gift for someone you don't know? And how could Billy buy a gift without any money?

Billy decided to ask Mum.

"Mum? What gift could I buy for the people that are going to be visiting school?" Billy asked.

"Oh, Billy. I'm not sure. Maybe you need to think carefully. We don't have any spare money to buy something," Mum answered.

Billy thought about that. Mum was right. They didn't have money to buy gifts. What was Billy going to do? Everyone was bringing gifts for the special day.

Later that week, Billy was at school and he was thinking about the special day. He was feeling sad because he still had not thought of a gift. Billy's teacher saw him sitting drawing at the drawing table. She noticed his sad face and slumped shoulders.

"Hi Billy," Miss Wombat said. "How are you feeling today?"

"I'm okay," Billy said with a sigh.

"You sound a bit sad, Billy," said Miss Wombat. "Is there something you would like to talk about?"

"Well," sighed Billy, "it's just that I'm really excited about buying a gift for our special visitors."

"Right?" said Miss Wombat. She knew that there was more to Billy's story.

"But I don't have any money to buy anything," Billy continued tearfully. "So maybe I can't come and meet the visitors."

Miss Wombat looked at Billy. She looked at the drawings that Billy had created. She smiled at Billy and her eyes shone.

"Why Billy," Miss Wombat said. "There is no need to buy a gift."

Billy looked up. Miss Wombat had his attention now. What did she mean?

"Billy, there are lots of ways we can give gifts. Sometimes we buy them, but sometimes we use our own gifts to bring joy to people."

Billy looked confused. He didn't have any gifts of his own to give.

Miss Wombat continued, "We all have our own special gifts that God picked out just for us. He knows us so well that He hand picks our gifts. Some people have the gift of growing pretty flowers and amazing fruits and vegetables. Others have the gift of handmaking toys and knitting clothes. And still others have the gift of knowing exactly when someone just needs a hug."

Billy thought about this. What was his gift? What had God picked out for him?

"Do you know what your gifts are Billy?" asked Miss Wombat.

"No…" said Billy. He looked at Miss Wombat hopefully. "Do you know, Miss Wombat?"

"Billy," said Miss Wombat smiling. "I can see one of your gifts right now. I'm looking at your drawing and I can see how great you are at creating a picture. Your flower looks so beautiful and real that it puts a smile on my face."

Billy looked at his drawing.

He thought about how he loved to draw. He thought about how happy Mum was when he drew something for her. He thought about how happy Grandpa was when he drew the picture of when they went fishing. Billy hadn't thought that his pictures were gifts. He didn't know that being able to draw was a gift from God. It made sense to him though. He knew God loved everyone so much! Being able to draw made him happy, and it made others happy.
Yes – being able to draw was a gift from God.

His gift from God.

Billy looked at his teacher and he hugged Miss Wombat.

"Thank you, Miss Wombat," Billy said. "Thank you for showing me my gift. I am going to draw a picture for our visitors. That will be my gift."

"That's a wonderful idea Billy," said Miss Wombat. "And Billy?"

"Yes, Miss Wombat?" said Billy.

"I think that giving hugs are one of your gifts too."

Billy smiled and got straight to work on his gift. He knew exactly what to draw!

Sharing your gift with others is special.

The End

About the Author and Illustrator

This is Cath and Victoria's first book together, both Author and Illustrator work in a very familiar setting known as kindy (kindergarten).

Author Cath La Rosa

Cath is a Teacher's Assistant who is passionate about helping children to identify their strengths. Living in the coastal town of Victoria Point, Queensland, she enjoys spending time with her family and taking walks along the beach. Creative writing for children is one of Cath's gifts.

Illustrator Victoria Carlsund

Originally from Sydney, the arts is a strong and integral part of Victoria's life. Her journey, with desire and passion to create something out of nothing, continues in Queensland with her family. Looking at the world in a creative way is Victoria's gift, a gift handed to her from her much admired and loving mother. Tori has over 20 years experience working with young children.

Gifts	Gifts	Gifts	Gifts	Gifts
Gifts	Gifts	Gifts	Gifts	Gifts
Gifts	Gifts	Gifts	Gifts	Gifts
Gifts	Gifts	Gifts	Gifts	Gifts
Gifts	Gifts	Gifts	Gifts	Gifts
Gifts	Gifts	Gifts	Gifts	Gifts
Gifts	Gifts	Gifts	Gifts	Gifts
Gifts	Gifts	Gifts	Gifts	Gifts
Gifts	Gifts	Gifts	Gifts	Gifts
Gifts	Gifts	Gifts	Gifts	Gifts

www.ingramcontent.com/pod-product-compliance
Lightning Source LLC
Chambersburg PA
CBHW061414090426
42742CB00023B/3466